MOLLY, ARCHITECT OF LIFE

MANIFESTATION? CHILD'S PLAY!

MOLLY
BOOK THREE

ANNA CAMILLA KUPKA

BUTTERFLY PUBLISHING

Butterfly Publishing – Anna Camilla Kupka
Zürich, Switzerland
Text: Anna Camilla Kupka
Illustrations: Carole Isler
Editor: Ursula Tanneberger
Translation: Doreen Zeitvogel
Copyright © 2023

Molly looks out the window and watches the snowflakes dancing in the air. It has been snowing non-stop for days, and the meadow outside her window looks like a bright white sheet.

Or like a fluffy white down comforter, thinks Molly. *A comforter made of clouds.*

All the same, Molly can't get enough of the sight. But now it has stopped snowing, and the sun has come out. Its rays are shining down, and every snow crystal is sparkling like a jewel. Sometimes the light flashes here, sometimes there—the sun's rays seem to skip from place to place. Molly's legs are tingling. She wants to get out and enjoy this fairytale landscape. To build a snowman, throw snowballs, and watch her breath form clouds in the air. Yes, she's going to do that now!

But first, there's something else she wants to know, a question that's been gnawing at her for days, and now she simply must have the answer. Otherwise, she won't be able to rest. And since she can't seem to figure it out on her own, she'll need a little help, which is why she now calls out into the room:

"Guardian angel, do you have a little time?"

Instantly, there's the sound of soft laughter. "What do you mean 'a little'? I have all the time in the world. So what's up?"

"Really? All the time in the world?" asks Molly,

amazed. "But I'm sure you have an awful lot to do. After all, there are a whole lot of us here."

"No, Molly," comes her guardian angel's cheery reply, "I'm here for you alone. Looking after you is my only job."

Molly is so dumbfounded she even forgets her question at first. "Isn't that a bit excessive?" she wants to know instead. "You could at least be responsible for a few other people. I can't be that much work."

"Why should we spread ourselves thin?" asks the guardian angel. "There are more than enough of us, so there's no need to cut corners. Besides, I'm really quite fond of you—I have no wish to be there for anyone else."

"I see," says Molly, smiling. In the meantime, she's grown fond of her guardian angel as well. But now she does want to get to her real concern.

"I have a question," she says, "but I'm not really sure how to put it. It all still feels a bit muddled in my head."

"Just give it a try," her guardian angel replies, encouraging her.

"Okay," says Molly, knitting her brow as she concentrates. Because what she wants to know is quite difficult to articulate. But then she begins:

"Recently, I've learned so much about myself and life, and I'm doing really well now, which is wonderful. But now, somehow—how do I put this—I don't know what to do with it all. You know, my father goes to work, but I have no idea if he even likes it or just why he does what he does. I go to school, and sometimes it's fun and sometimes not. With some subjects, I honestly don't know why I need to learn those things—they just seem so pointless. On the other hand, I love to sing, but I can't just sing all day. So what should I do? What should I focus on? I'm already trying to let love be my guide, but it's so incredibly vast, I think I sometimes get lost in it all."

"Aha, I think I understand you, Molly," her guardian angel says with his pleasant laugh. "You're basically asking about the meaning of human existence. Wow, you ask some questions! Next time, I'll pick a protégé who ponders a little less," he teases, and Molly can tell he doesn't really mean it.

The guardian angel continues:

"No, really, Molly, that's quite a complex question for a teenager. In fact, a lot of adults never even consider it. But I'll try to explain it to you, and I can already tell you: the meaning of human existence is quite wonderful, so that's something to be happy about."

Molly is beaming now. She's glad she brought up the topic, and now she's waiting to have the solution to the puzzle handed to her on a silver platter. Having such a wise guardian angel by your side is really very useful.

But rather than giving her a satisfying answer, he suggests: "You know what? You wanted to go outside and play a little. How about we do that first?"

"Oh, all right," Molly answers, a bit disappointed. Still, if her guardian angel is always by her side and feels like going outside right now, then she doesn't want to let him down. It's probably also boring for him to sit here with her all day long and watch her go back and forth between singing and staring at snowflakes. *And pondering, too,* she thinks. And so she goes to the wardrobe, pulls on her winter boots and warm jacket, and then her hat and gloves, and she's ready to go. She calls out a quick "Bye!" to her mother, and she's already out the door and right in the white, snowy landscape.

It's now started to snow a little again, and Molly looks up at the sky, laughing. She opens her mouth wide and sticks out her tongue. She loves to catch the flakes with her tongue and watch them melt. And she loves to feel the cool snowflakes on her face. Her guardian angel was right about going outside, after all. All this thinking is nothing compared to being out in the fresh air and feeling the snow on her skin!

Full of joy, Molly begins to build a snowman. Not an especially big one—more like a baby snowman, but she finds him awfully cute and christens him Kasimir. Then she dashes back into the house to get a carrot from the kitchen. As she's running out, she hears her mother scolding her because she tracked slush into the house. But right now, Molly doesn't care. Besides, Kasimir needs a nose. So Molly sticks the carrot on his face, makes two eyes and a mouth with a few round stones she found on the way, and then races back into the house to fetch a small pot from the kitchen for a hat. Once again, she neglected to take off her boots, and now she'd better run out in a flash because her mother is coming after her. She's apparently not too thrilled to have water all over the floor.

But then two children, who happen to be walking by with their parents, are thrilled to pieces and loudly proclaiming their delight over Kasimir. The neighbor, too, calls out: "Nice snowman, Molly. I hope he stays up for a while!" Molly waves and can feel how her cheeks are burning despite the cold.

"Come on, let's go for a walk," she mentally says to her guardian angel. "Maybe we'll find a couple more snowmen along the way." And with that, she bids Kasimir farewell with a playful bow and merrily skips away.

"Hang on, Molly, not so fast," her guardian angel calls out after her. "Before we forget it entirely, with the snowman, you just gave yourself the answer to your question."

"Which question?" Molly calls back politely, though she's far more interested in bounding through the snow and reveling in the fresh footprints she's left in the virtually untouched landscape.

"You asked me what people live for, and you just answered it yourself."

"All I did was build a snowman," Molly says, laughing. "That can hardly be what we're all meant to be doing here. If it were, there would be a whole lot of snowmen in the world."

"No, not everyone needs to build a snowman—that's true." Her guardian angel is also laughing now. "But you did much more than that. You had the idea for a snowman, then you were seized with the wish to build it, and poof!—you created it. You made your wish come true. And that's basically what people are here to do: to live their dreams. Building a snowman is also fulfilling a dream. Even if it's not a particularly big one, especially since Kasimir turned out a bit puny. But everyone starts small," the guardian angel says cheerfully.

Molly has no interest in arguing about Kasimir's size just now. She'd rather get to the heart of the matter. "People are here to live their dreams?" she asks with a skeptical look. "Are you sure about that? That sounds a bit odd to me. And a little too simple."

"Yes, I'm quite sure about that," her guardian angel replies, laughing. "Birds sing, rivers flow, the sun shines, and people manifest their dreams."

"Mani… what? What kind of word is that?" Molly asks, perplexed. "I've never heard that before." At the same time, though, she's a little relieved. If there's something complicated like this "mani" word behind it, then her guardian angel is more likely to be right. Life is complicated, after all. Surely, it can't be as simple as living your dreams.

"Oh, sorry, Molly," the guardian angel replies in his usual cheerful way. "So to manifest means to make something come true. You have a vision inside you, an idea, a dream, and then you give expression to that dream and make it a reality. Ideally, it's something that brings joy to you and others, just as Kasimir brought joy not just to you but also to the children walking by and to your neighbor."

"Although Mom didn't seem that thrilled with

him," Molly murmurs, but she decides to believe her guardian angel for now. "But then it's pretty simple," she continues. "We're all supposed to be doing something all day long."

The whole thing is starting to make sense to her now. Having something to do seems extremely important—that's something she's noticed again and again. Adults, in particular, seem to take this very seriously. "So it's like Dad working all day, after all," she concludes. "Then he's doing exactly the right thing."

"It's not quite like that either, Molly. What matters most is the driving force behind the activity, or why you do what you do. And whether it makes you happy. Activity, for activity's sake alone, accomplishes little and can feel rather empty. Or exhausting. That's not really the point, and it doesn't usually lead to the desired result—but we'll get to that. For now, let's keep walking."

"All right," says Molly and skips away once more.

Along the way, Molly sings happily to herself while bending over again and again to make snowballs and then throw them as far as she can. As she does this, she's thinking: Could it really be as simple as her guardian angel says? She still can't quite believe it and doesn't understand it, either. But from what she knows of her guardian angel by now, he will eventually explain it better.

And once again, his voice rings out: "Here we have a good example, Molly. Who is your school named after?"

Molly looks up, confused. She was so busy thinking she didn't even notice she had made her way to school —even though it's Saturday today. But now she's standing right before it.

She answers immediately. "Well, it's named after the man who built it. He must have been really famous. He built several of the buildings in town, including the town hall," Molly declares, proud of her knowledge.

"That's right. He was the architect. That's what they call someone who designs buildings."

Molly knows that, too. Her uncle is an architect, but to be honest, she was never exactly sure of what he did. So now she listens with interest. Then, maybe next time, she can show off a bit in front of him.

"And this architect, Molly, how did he build this school here or the town hall? Did he pull up in a giant truck loaded with bricks, dump them out, pile them on top of each other, and then simply watch the building take shape before his eyes?"

Molly has to laugh. "No, of course not. He must have first created a plan. Otherwise, he wouldn't even know what he wanted to build."

"Aha," says the guardian angel. "You mean a plan on a piece of paper? So he took a pencil, simply drew on the pad, and then was amazed to see this exact building take shape on the paper? Is that how it was?"

"No, he must have first thought about how the building should look and then drawn it. My uncle always gets really excited when a building appears in his mind's eye. 'Flashes of inspiration' like that, as my father calls them, can come at any moment. Or sometimes, when my uncle is visiting us, he'll suddenly sit down to doodle on the sketch pad he always has with him, and then no one is allowed to disturb him. I think at those times he actually sees the building in front of him—completely built. With colors and shutters and the whole works."

Her guardian angel agrees: "Yes, and then getting the building down on paper is no longer so hard, is it? And then maybe he'll build a model and finally the whole building. But he created the building inside himself before it could take shape on the outside. And it works exactly the same way for you: you are the architect of your own life, Molly. You imagine your life, and then you create it. Everything starts with a dream."

Molly thinks back to her mother's mental world. She imagined Rome and Florence in her mind's eye, and then she and Molly actually booked a trip to Italy for the spring. Her mother first created the wish in her mind, and now it was becoming a reality.

It's exactly the same as how her mother first imagines the pictures she paints and then puts them on canvas. As she always explains: "I can literally see them in my mind." And then she gets frustrated when she can't reproduce the image precisely as she imagined it. But the more she practices, the better she gets.

It's also the same with Molly when she sings. Before the sounds come out, they've already formed within her. She knows exactly what she wants to hear. Maybe her guardian angel really is right, although Molly is still a little skeptical.

"Okay," she says, "but I still don't understand. You mean we're supposed to dream and then create? Sounds pretty simple. That's it?"

"You want to know if that's it?" the guardian angel asks in an incredulous tone. "Molly, creating something is like a miracle, and yet you do nothing else all day and act like it's natural. You create your life with every moment, every second. You can't help it. Everything you do and experience is a creation of yours. You want to lift your arm, and that immediately sets millions of processes in motion inside you so that you can lift it. You don't have to think about it at all. You want to say something, and you say it. You want to sing, and you sing. You want to throw a snowball, and you do that, too. You want to turn on the light, so you flip a switch, and from what was a room full of darkness before, you create a room filled with brightness—or even an entire stadium, if you want. Poof! And you do it like it's nothing. With every single second, you are creating your world. What you see around you is the result of your creative process. And you ask: That's it? What more in heaven's name could you possibly want?"

"Well, that's great then, because in that case I'm already doing exactly what I'm supposed to be doing," Molly replies, a little petulant and somewhat disappointed by the answer. As she says this, she quietly moves one arm up and down. *So what's so great about that?* she thinks.

"Well, there's actually more to it than that," her guardian angel answers. "Because, as you can see, you do all this more or less automatically. You just take it for granted. But the point is to do it all consciously, to be conscious of your creative power, and to create the life you want to live—a life that makes your heart sing. Love would be very pleased with that because it wants its beloved creation, human beings, to be happy. As you know, everything comes from Love, animals, nature, and all things, but of all its creations, only you humans can create consciously. And you can create exactly the life you want! This is a sacred gift, and you treat what's in fact a divine power like nothing special. But by creating unconsciously, you're wasting your potential. You really should make the most of it, Molly!"

Molly is thinking. It's true. She can, in fact, design her own life—at least, up to a point. But surely not everything. Living her dreams just like that still sounds too simple to her. Even so, she decides to follow her guardian angel's train of thought for the time being. Something interesting may still come of it.

"And how am I supposed to do this? The way you put it, all I have to do is imagine something and it happens."

"Yes, because when you make a wish, the universe gives you whatever you need to make the wish come true. But for that to happen, you need to visualize exactly what you want, really see it in front of you, and feel it. You want your whole emotional world to fuel your mental fireworks and send them out into the universe full of energy. And when the universe knows exactly what you want, then it gives you that. It's like Aladdin and the magic lamp: your wish is the universe's command. But you must communicate your wish correctly, so the universe knows what to give you."

"Hmmm," replies Molly, doubtful. So far, the universe has cared relatively little about what she wants, no matter how much she communicated her wishes. But now she's done enough thinking for the moment.

"I'm thirsty," she says. "Come on, let's go get a lemonade at Mrs. Sullivan's shop." Just the thought of lemonade is making her mouth water.

"That's a great idea, Molly. I can show you what I mean right now. Let's play a game. You're not going to simply order a lemonade from Mrs. Sullivan. Instead, you'll repeat everything I say, okay?"

"If you say so," Molly says, hesitating. What is her guardian angel up to now? But by then, they've already arrived at the small general store, which Molly quickly enters.

"Good afternoon, Mrs. Sullivan," she says gaily, "I'd like a ..."

But before she can utter the word "lemonade," she hears her guardian angel whisper: "Stop! You were only supposed to repeat what I said to you."

Oh, right, Molly thinks, having completely forgotten about the game.

"Good afternoon, Molly," Mrs. Sullivan says warmly. "What would you like? A piece of chocolate, perhaps?"

"No, no chocolate today, Mrs. Sullivan, thank you. I would like ..." *What am I supposed to say now?* Molly mentally asks her guardian angel.

"A drink," comes the whispered voice of the guardian angel. "Say you want a drink."

That's not very precise, Molly thinks in reply. *How is Mrs. Sullivan supposed to know what I want?*

Mrs. Sullivan is now looking at her expectantly. Molly would rather just order her lemonade, but she knows that her guardian angel can be very stubborn, so she plays along.

"A drink," Molly dutifully answers, already feeling slightly silly. Usually, she always knows exactly what she wants. It's not at all her style to be so vague.

Pleasant as always, Mrs. Sullivan replies, "Well, we have quite a few, Molly. What kind of drink would you like?"

"A refreshing one," says the guardian angel, and Molly repeats "A refreshing one."

Now Mrs. Sullivan is looking a little surprised, but she remains friendly. Inwardly, however, she's wondering: *What's wrong with Molly today? The girl is not herself at all. I hope she's not getting sick—her cheeks are really quite flushed. Usually, she's not so hesitant.*

To Molly, she says, "We have lots of those as well: water, juice, soda. Would you like an iced tea perhaps?"

Molly shudders. She doesn't like iced tea at all. "A lemonade, please," she now replies. She's had enough of this game.

But it's apparently not yet over because Mrs. Sullivan now asks her: "Lemon or orange?"

Once again, Molly no longer waits for her guardian angel's answer. Instead, she firmly states: "Lemon." But even that is not enough. She still has to decide whether she wants the small or large bottle and with or without sugar. She never realized how much information a simple purchase would take. But in the end, she counted out her change, laid it down, got the large lemonade with no sugar from Mrs. Sullivan, and is now standing in the fresh air again with her guardian angel.

"What was that about?" she asks, slightly annoyed.

"That was just what happens when you want something but don't know exactly what it is. Or you know what you want but don't communicate it properly. How is the universe supposed to know what to give you if you're not specific with what you say? If you had walked in and said, 'Mrs. Sullivan, I'd like a lemonade of such and such brand, the big bottle, please, with no sugar and ice cold,' she would have given you the right thing straight away. The whole operation would have taken less than a minute. A picture would have immediately formed in her head, and you would have gotten the bottle you wanted immediately. With how things went, though, she had to literally round up the information. Now imagine if you had not told her what you wanted but shown her a picture instead. In one split second, she would have known what you wanted without the need for further explanation and with little room for misunderstanding. She would not have first offered you an iced tea, which you don't like at all.

That's how it works with the universe, too. It wants to give you everything you want, but for that, you need to be precise. And the best way to do that is to imagine things precisely, like showing the universe a picture. Then the universe knows exactly what you want and can send it to you just as you want it."

Molly has to laugh. She can't help thinking of Peter from her class, who, as a little boy, had asked his parents for a yellow toy Jeep for Christmas. But since he had quite a lisp at the time, his parents understood that he wanted a sieve, which they were happy to give him, though they were somewhat surprised as well. Peter described to the class his bitter disappointment when, as a small child, he eagerly unwrapped his gift, only to find a yellow plastic sieve instead of the Jeep he so fervently desired. *At least the color was right,* Molly thinks with a laugh. In this regard, her guardian angel was correct. If Peter had shown his parents a picture, the misunderstanding would never have happened.

"Visualization, Molly, is what it's called when you see in your mind's eye how you want something to look. It's the same as showing the universe a picture. And it works best when you not only see it but feel it, when you imagine yourself in the exact situation you desire and can literally feel what it will be like once you realize your dream."

Molly thinks back to her experience just now with the lemonade and how it made her mouth water just to think about it. She could feel exactly what it would be like to have the refreshing drink gliding down her throat.

"That's right, Molly, because when you can really feel it, your whole emotional world comes alive and gives your thoughts a mighty puff to fill them up with steam. That way, they get the stuff they need to soar into the heights as fireworks and go out into the universe."

Molly's eyes sparkle. She remembers the journey into her inner life when she imagined herself onstage as a successful singer. That had felt wonderful, and the fireworks had shot right up—farther even than she could see, past the moon and the stars. But then she remembers some thoughts that didn't feel so good, that made her feel small. They had very little rocketlike energy. Her feelings apparently had no desire to feed those thoughts with energy. Molly was not surprised. After all, who wants to waste their energy on something negative, something they *don't* want?

"Exactly, Molly," her guardian angel concurs. "All the colors of the fireworks are fed by your feelings. That's where they get their vibrancy. And as you know, the more Love can flow freely through your feelings, the more vivid, colorful, and energized they become. Then everything really gets going and the fireworks truly blaze. That's also why your good thoughts have so much more power than your negative ones. But the negative ones can still get in the way quite a bit."

That's true, thinks Molly, recalling how the negative thoughts hung around the universe like air pollution and made it harder for the pleasant ones to get through. *So it's best not to feed those thoughts and to just imagine what you want—to visu... visu... What's that called again?* Another one of those difficult words her guardian angel taught her.

He immediately comes to her rescue. "Visualize, Molly. That's what it's called. And the other word was manifest."

"Ugh, so many hard words today," says Molly.

"The words themselves are not so important in this case. But when you break it down, 'visualize' comes from 'vision,' so something you see in front of you. And 'manifest' comes from *manus,* which means 'hand' in Latin and refers to creating something outside yourself. This is a natural process: you see something in front of your mind's eye, or you have a vision, which means that you're already creating it internally, and then the universe brings you everything you need to carry it over to the outside. So that's the way it always works: from the inside out. The outside world is a reflection of your inner world. And that's what people are here for: to turn their visions into reality!"

Oh, so that's how it works, thinks Molly. Then she bends down, forms a snowball with her hands, and throws it at the school wall. And then another. And another. It's fun to watch the snowballs burst apart, leaving only a white splotch on the wall. And now she understands a little better what her guardian angel means: The desire to make a snowball arises within her, so she does it. It first appears as an image inside her—a vision; and then outside—the manifestation. Even though it's Saturday, she feels like she's in school today with all the new things she's learning!

"Yes, well, that's all fine, dear guardian angel," Molly now counters. "But surely it only works for little things. Like when I ask Mrs. Sullivan for a lemonade, of course, I get it. After all, it's her job to sell me lemonade, so naturally, she's glad when customers come. Or when I want to make a snowball. But what if I want something big or lots of money? I wouldn't get it just like that."

"Ha!" laughs the guardian angel. "It is Mrs. Sullivan's job to give you a lemonade, and it's the universe's job to give you whatever you want, no matter how big your wish. Love has entrusted the universe with this task because when people live their dreams, Love experiences itself in all its marvelous facets and can enjoy more and more new creations. That's why the universe will give you everything you need to make your dreams come true. It's been hitting you in the face all along, Molly. Just look around. Look at the snow, the sun, and the whole of nature around you. With all that splendor, how can you still believe the universe is stingy? It gives you plenty of snow, plenty of sunlight, and all the air you can breathe. When you sing, every tone in the world is present within you, and your mother can paint every color in the spectrum. And you all have your own guardian angel, no matter how small you are or insignificant you feel—and you think the universe is holding back as far as giving you what you want? Or that anything is too big for it? It causes storms to sweep the land, making the air vibrate, and the seas boil. It makes the sun, the moon, and the stars appear in the sky... and it's too weak to fulfill your wishes? No, Molly, no matter what you desire, it's easy as pie for the universe. In fact, the universe loves it when you think big! You can never think big enough! That's when it can really play with you and show you what it can do! Don't put a lid on your desires, Molly. Let them blossom, grow, and send sparks up to the sky. Challenge the universe! And you'll see: it will always answer you because it loves to play, and it's elated when someone recognizes its true size. Then it gives and gives and gives, just to show you what it can do. The universe is like a giant sweet shop with simply everything. No matter what you want from this shop, it's as easy for the universe to give it to you as it is for Mrs. Sullivan to give you a bottle of lemonade! Help yourself from this store, Molly—help yourself as much as you want, and enjoy it!"

"Hmmm," says Molly, her eyes sparkling at the idea of a giant sweet shop just for her. But then she gets realistic again: "That sounds almost too good to be true. Because you really can't say that it always works. I've wished for things hundreds of times and not gotten them—I can't tell you how many times." Molly sighs and thinks of the countless conversations she's had with her parents when she wanted something but didn't get it, no matter how much she begged and whined.

Her guardian angel laughs. Molly doesn't know what there is to laugh about. After all, she just showed him that he's also wrong sometimes, didn't she? Surely, even her guardian angel has reached the limits of his capacity now.

But he's not about to be silenced so quickly.

"Let's take a closer look at this, too, Molly," he says. "For you humans, it's very important to understand everything with your mind. And for your mind to classify and understand things better, Love has made everything on earth subject to definite natural laws. Do you know what a law of nature is?"

Molly thinks of her physics class, where this phrase came up again and again. And although she didn't understand it all by any stretch of the imagination, she still gives a hesitant answer: "I'm not sure, but I think it's something like a rule. A rule that always holds and that wasn't established by humans but by nature."

"That's right," says the guardian angel, obviously proud of his protégé's knowledge. "A law of nature is a rule of the universe. There is no chaos in nature, you see. Rather, there's an all-encompassing order, though this is not always immediately apparent to humans. But clever people who call themselves natural scientists work tirelessly to understand these rules. Because then they can calculate and predict things. For example, if you throw a snowball and the natural scientist knows how heavy the snowball is, the speed at which it flies, and the angle at which it's thrown, then he can calculate exactly where and with how much force the snowball will land. Or what happens, Molly, when you jump up in the air, for example?"

"Then I fly really far away," Molly says, her eyes shining. "No, no," she corrects herself with a wink, "then I hit the ground again, but hopefully not too hard."

And with that, she leaps up, laughing, and falls backward onto the soft snow. Then she jumps back up, makes a few snowballs, and throws them at the school wall with oomph.

"That's right, Molly," the guardian angel agrees, laughing. "It's a law of nature that you land back down on the ground. And now imagine if I told you that sometimes you come back down when you jump up and sometimes you don't. Or that sometimes the snowballs explode on the wall, and sometimes they don't. That what happens is pure chance. You'd think I was pretty stupid then, wouldn't you?"

"Well, naïve, at least," Molly answers, laughing.

"And rightly so. Yet isn't it strange how we say that sometimes wishes come true and sometimes not? Where do the laws of nature cease to apply, and where does witchcraft or mere chance begin? Nowhere, of course! Our wishes, like everything else, are governed by the laws of the universe. When the right conditions are fulfilled, then every wish will also be fulfilled! Many people still don't understand that, but that doesn't change the fact that it's true."

Molly is now listening with interest. She is no longer bored and can't wait to find out what comes next. It's almost like she's learning how to perform miracles!

"Of course, everything happens in its own time," the guardian angel continues, "for the laws of nature govern that as well. You can wish all you want to make snowballs in the summer. Your wish will be granted but not until winter, when there's snow again. Or you do know that in the summertime there's always a beautiful blossoming meadow here."

Molly smiles. Yes, the meadow is lovely.

"Right now, you don't see the meadow at all—it's covered with snow. But even if there were no snow, you wouldn't see any flowers simply because the time for them is not yet ripe. And yet, beyond our sight, beneath the earth and unnoticed by us, the buds are once more preparing to break through the soil with the sun's first warm rays—and, finally, to bloom. It would be useless, though, if you came here every day right now and waited during winter for the flowers to appear. No matter how much you watch and wait, the flowers simply don't come up in the winter. You would probably lose faith that they would ever bloom again. But they're just waiting for their time, and they will appear when the time is right. The same holds true for you. You wished with lots of positive energy to be onstage as a famous singer. Although you're not yet famous, you received a gift of singing lessons a short while later. They may be needed to become a great singer, just as sun and water are needed for buds to blossom. Everything comes at the right time, Molly. Love is watching carefully, and by and large, it's all perfectly ordered and endlessly bountiful and playful."

"Oh, I see," Molly says now. "I think I understand. So then I'm supposed to imagine exactly what I want, provide the wish with the right energy to rise up to the heavens, and then trust that it will come true in its own time. Is that right?"

"Very good, Molly, that's exactly right," says the guardian angel.

"You said the universe will then give me everything I need to fulfill my wish, but what does that mean? Do I still have to work hard for it? Probably, right? Not everything happens on its own, after all. Even you can't claim that."

"Oh, no? Can't I?" the guardian angel asks her, teasing. "You can see that today is full of surprises because I think I'm now going to claim just that. Do the flowers need to work hard to bloom? Do the birds have to struggle and strain to sing? Does the snow need to toil in order to fall, or the sun have to labor and sweat to shine? Does it say every morning: 'Ugh, I really don't feel like shining right now. I wish I could do something else.' No, like everything else in nature, it carries out its intended purpose and does so quite naturally and effortlessly. And since human beings are also part of nature and it's their natural purpose to live their dreams, some action is often needed along the way—no question about that. But it should always be playful and have a certain lightness and joy. When you built Kasimir, your cheeks were flushed from the work, but it was work you enjoyed. When your brother plays football, afterwards he's totally out of breath and panting, but he feels fulfilled. When you sing, you sometimes feel frustration when you miss a note, but the underlying joy that comes from singing is still there within you. Or when you keep throwing those blasted snowballs at the wall, every muscle in your arm has to tense up and perform at its utmost capacity, which you could certainly call hard work. Still, you obviously think it's loads of fun... which is why I hope your arm gets tired soon. At any rate, I'm already pretty dazed from all this pounding."

Molly laughs as she slams another snowball against the wall. "Or the way the buds poke their heads through the earth to get to the surface," she says, completing the train of thought. "It does involve some work, but it also happens naturally and sort of casually. Yeah, I guess you're right."

"Exactly," her guardian angel replies, agreeing. "Because life is a process of unfolding, not a struggle. When your actions feel good and natural, then you're in tune with the universe."

"But what if my wish doesn't come true after all?" asks Molly. "Even if I visualize a whole lot?" She feels proud to have pronounced this difficult word without any problem.

"Then trust that Love has a good reason for that and that it always wants what's best for you. It's like the time your mother kept you from jumping off the barn roof when you were a little girl, even though you wanted to so badly. If your wish doesn't come true, that's a good thing, too."

"Well, great," says Molly, "you wriggled your way

out of that one gracefully: it always works out, but when it doesn't, you can be glad." She laughs. "It's like the joker in a card game. But I bet there's a catch to it. Because if it were really that easy, everyone would be doing it and living their dream life."

"The only catch, Molly, is the one you've already seen yourself. It's the dark clouds that just love to block your desires, the belittling thoughts that usually come in the form of doubt. They can really get in the way of fulfilling your wishes because they stop the wishes from freely rising to the heavens. It's like rolling a marble and suddenly finding a pebble in the way."

"So that's why wishes fail to come true?" asks Molly. "Because of doubt?"

"Yes, doubting thoughts are the biggest reason why people sometimes fail to live their dreams. Why do you think some people achieve a lot and others not so much? The difference in most cases is that those who achieve a lot have no doubt that their dreams will come true. Often, their upbringing was such that they had already received a lot. As a result, they take it for granted that their wishes will be fulfilled. They simply have more trust in the universe. And that makes it easier to take whatever actions are needed to make their dreams come true, because doubt isn't always butting in and dragging them back down. Doubters, on the other hand, tend to forget who they are. They forget that by their very nature, they are the source of all things, and all things are available to them. And Love would like you all to remember how infinitely rich and splendid you are."

"Oh, yes, doubt; you're right about that," Molly moans. "I'm familiar with that, too. When I sing, I'm sometimes unsure if I've hit the right note—and poof, I'm off the mark."

"Exactly. But the more you practice, the better you get. And you know why? Because then you gain faith. Faith that the right notes will come to you. Faith that everything you need is already within you. And faith is the opposite of doubt. So, Molly, fill your dreams with joy and faith, and don't let them waste away by weighing them down with doubt."

"Yes, doubt can really interfere and drain your energy. But what should I do about it? Simply trusting just like that is not that easy."

"Although it should be that easy," her guardian angel replies, sighing. "But you all were raised to not trust the universe, to mistakenly assume that life is a struggle. There's a difficult word for that, too, but I'll spare you that for today. Anyway, I have good news, Molly! There's an incredibly simple and powerful trick, but very few people know it. It even works when you don't know exactly what to wish for but still want to live a happy life. Should I tell you what it is?"

"Yes, please!" Molly answers, her eyes sparkling. She feels like a big secret is about to be revealed.

The guardian angel clears his throat. He evidently has something important to tell her. "When you want something, what do you say?" her guardian angel now asks her.

"Well, then I say *please*, of course," replies Molly, somewhat baffled by this question. "Just as I did now. Just as my parents taught me. And if I ever forget— boy, am I in for a treat." She rolls her eyes.

Her guardian angel laughs. "Yes, that's how most children feel, and it is polite to say *please*. And what do you say when you're given something?"

Molly feels a bit like she's back in kindergarten with these questions. "Then I say *thank you*," she answers, anyway.

"Right, and don't worry, it's about to get a bit harder. What's the difference between *please* and *thank you*?"

Molly thinks it over. She says *please* beforehand and *thank you* afterwards, but that can't be what her guardian angel means. That would be too easy. She imagines herself in a situation where she asks her parents for something and then thanks them afterwards. Like with her singing lessons—she tries to remember how she felt. And she recalls that in the past, she often tried to persuade her parents to let her take singing lessons. Then she would stand in front of them, repeatedly saying *please* and sometimes even pressing her hands together in front of her chest while knitting her brows. That would make her feel cramped inside because she would feel quite desperate and didn't really believe her parents would grant her wish. But then, when her mother gave her singing lessons out of the blue, everything opened up inside, her face was beaming, and she thanked her.

"Ha, I think I've got it," she says. "When I say *please*, I still have doubts. I don't know if I'll actually get what I want, and I feel unsure. But when I say *thank you*, I already have it. All my doubts are gone, and a huge feeling of joy wells up inside me. Then I'm so happy I could dance." And with that, she gleefully twirls about a couple of times.

"That's right, Molly," says her guardian angel, and Molly can hear the sparkle in his voice. "Gratitude and doubt are mutually exclusive. When you create a state of gratitude, you vibrate with joy and faith. This is at once the most powerful and most natural state you can experience. And what does the universe do, then? It sends you more and more to be thankful for—always more and more. Even things you hadn't thought of before but that still fill you with gratitude. Because there's another law, Molly, and it's this: like attracts like. Radiate thankfulness, and you will always have more to be thankful for."

Molly nods, her eyes wide. She's never viewed

things quite like this before. But what should she do now? "Should I always say *thank you* instead of *please*?" she asks uncertainly. "That would sound a bit strange, wouldn't it?"

"That's true," the guardian angel acknowledges, laughing. "But by now, we know that the crucial thing is your inner life and not so much the outside world, which is only a reflection of your inner life. So inside yourself, you can absolutely be in a state of thankfulness as often as possible. Because look, the moment you imagine something, you've already created it. You see it before you. You feel how it feels. Often, you can even practically smell and taste it. So what more do you want? Replicating it in the outside world is a breeze if that's all that's left to do. Inside you, where the real power lies, it's already come about! Which means that you can safely give thanks that your wish will come true. This deprives every doubting thought of its power. And if in the beginning it seems unnatural to give thanks for things that have only happened inside you so far, then start by expressing your thanks for the little outward things. Be thankful for the snow and the sun today, that you can run around outside and make snowballs, that just now you could enjoy a lemonade—for all that. And when you don't know exactly what to think, just think of all the things you can be thankful for. This is the best way to clear out all doubt and draw more good into your life. And then your path will open up before you."

"And what, guardian angel, is my path?"

"It's the path of your heart, of course. Whatever your heart desires deep down inside. And the more you live in the energy of gratitude, the more clearly your heart's desire will not only reveal itself but also—and here's that word again—manifest. So just open your heart in gratitude, and soon you'll no longer be confused. Step by step, your path will naturally open up before you."

"I want to be a singer," Molly says while looking dreamily into the distance.

"Then don't let doubt deter you from that path but be thankful for every opportunity you have to sing. And now you can even be thankful for school. Because if you hadn't learned to read there, you wouldn't be able to read the lyrics to your songs. Be grateful for the talent you've been given. By the way, everyone has a talent. Many people simply don't realize it. It's usually what brings you the most joy. It's wonderful that you recognized yours so early."

Another reason to be thankful, Molly thinks to herself, smiling.

And now she understands: If Love is our true nature and the source of all things, then all of us are infinitely rich. We just need to draw from this wealth and bring it into the world.

And with that, in the snow-covered meadow, Molly begins to sing a song that rises up within her, takes on form, and then breaks out in clear, bright tones—to her own delight and to the delight of everyone who can hear it.

ALSO BY ANNA CAMILLA KUPKA

Molly's Wondrous Journey

Molly Enchants Her World

Molly, Architect of Life

Ticket to Earth and Back

Printed in Great Britain
by Amazon

37631221R00025